S0-AGL-904

RAY CHARLES

RAY CHARLES

SHARON BELL MATHIS
ILLUSTRATED BY GEORGE FORD

Lee & Low Books Inc.
New York

This book is for
my father, John W. Bell, Sr., tenor;
my brother, John W. Bell, Jr., baritone;
my grandsons, Thomas Kevin Allen II, rapper, and James Madison Diggs III;
my great grandson, Tarron Christopher Allen;
my uncle, Richard Henry Frazier, tenor;
my nephews, John W. Bell III and Terrance Heyward;
my son-in-law, Malcolm Xavier Hamilton, guitarist,
former linebacker, the Washington Redskins;
six precious infants, now grown into manhood, and still precious:
William Kenneth Gross, Jr.,
Brian Jerome Makell, Stephen Anthony Makell, William Joseph Makell, Jr.,
twins Gary Douglas Snowden and Gregory Lloyd Snowden.
All of you are *music* in my life!
— *S.B.M.*

For my daughter Olivia, a creative spirit
with an infectious personality — like Ray Charles!
— *G.F.*

Text copyright © 2001, 1973 by Sharon Bell Mathis
Illustrations copyright © 1973 by George Ford
All rights reserved. No part of the contents of this book may be reproduced
by any means without the written permission of the publisher.
LEE & LOW BOOKS Inc., 95 Madison Avenue, New York, NY 10016
www.leeandlow.com

Printed in China

Book design by Tania Garcia
Book production by The Kids at Our House

The text is set in 14 pt. Goudy Old Style.
The illustrations are rendered in acrylic and India ink on extra rough illustration board.

10 9 8 7 6 5 4 3 2
First LEE & LOW Edition, 2001

   The author wishes to express gratitude, with hugs, to the following individuals for initial and current research assistance during the writing of this book: Joseph Allen ("blues man"), teacher, Baltimore, Maryland; Cathryn Baker, Sickle Cell Disease Association of America, Los Angeles, California; Constance Barber, retired librarian, and Constance Jackson, retired special education teacher, Charles Hart Junior High School, Washington, DC; Marcia C. Bell and Jacqueline Washington, Orlando, Florida; Shirley Edwards Gross, Technical Services, Community College of Southern Maryland; Helena Nobles Jones, Principal, Charles Herbert Flowers High School, Capital Heights, Maryland; Angela Mason, Center for Sickle Cell Disease, Washington, DC; Stacy Mathis-Collins, Sherie Mathis Diggs, and Stephanie Mathis-Hamilton (student, Howard University); Pam Hamlin, Josephine Hobbs-Ford, Jean Massey, Marsha Quarles, Tata Scholtz, Teresa Stakem, and Brenda Williams, library media specialists, Oxon Hill Branch, Prince George's County, Maryland, Memorial Library System; John Theodore Whitney for transportation to/assistance at the Schomburg Center for Research in Black Culture, New York Public Library; and Jackie Perkins, Montsho Books, Orlando, Florida.
   The author is also grateful to Time/Life Syndication Service for permission to use material from the text of "Music Soaring in a Darkened World" by Thomas Thompson, *Life* magazine, © 1966 Time, Inc.

Library of Congress Cataloging-in-Publication Data
Mathis, Sharon Bell.
    Ray Charles / by Sharon Bell Mathis ; illustrated by George Ford.— 1st. ed.
       p.   cm.
    ISBN 1-58430-017-5
    1. Charles, Ray, 1930—Juvenile literature. 2. Singers—United States—Biography—Juvenile literature.
[1. Charles, Ray, 1930- 2. Musicians. 3. Afro-Americans—Biography. 4. Blind. 5. Physically handicapped.]
I. Ford, George Cephas ill. II. Title.
ML3930.C443 M42 2001   782.42164'092—dc21   [B]   00-064109

Free Teacher's Guide available at www.leeandlow.com/teachers

WHEN this book was first published in 1973, Ray Charles was already a famous musician, respected by people all around the world and from all walks of life. But the journey Ray Charles took to stardom was long and hard and very much influenced by the economic and racial conditions in the United States during the 1930s and 1940s.

Ray Charles was born in 1930 at the beginning of the Great Depression. His family had very little money, and they lived amid discrimination that made daily life even more difficult for African Americans at the time. In spite of their circumstances, Ray's mother, Retha Robinson, was determined to help her young son succeed in life. Although she could do nothing to save his eyesight, she did nurture in Ray a strong desire for knowledge, learning, and self-sufficiency. She encouraged her son to persevere during hard times, explore new ideas and ways to do things, and make plans for the future. She told him to follow his dreams, no matter how difficult the path or how long the road.

When Retha Robinson had taught Ray all she knew, it was time for others to help. "Mind your teachers, son!" she said as she placed the seven-year-old boy aboard a train headed for St. Augustine School for the Blind.

And so began Ray Charles' journey to stardom.

Sharon Bell Mathis, 2001

"**HEY, FOOTS!**" a boy yelled. He was on the Black children's side of the wire that ran down the yard of St. Augustine School for the Blind.

"Hey, Foots! Hey, Ray — Ray Charles Robinson! Come on and race!"

The barefoot boy, called Foots because he had no shoes, had arrived at the school only a few days before.

Ray stood still and thought for a moment.

He wasn't thinking of his blindness. That didn't matter. It had never stopped him from doing exactly what he wanted.

Ray wanted to run a perfect race. He was thinking of how to win.

Once his mother had held him close.

"You're blind," she said, "not stupid. You lost your sight, not your mind."

Suddenly he knew how to do it. He knew how to win.

A child stood at each end of the wire, pulling it tight. All Ray had to do was grab the wire at the starting point and follow it to the end.

But he didn't grab the wire. His small, seven-year-old fingers felt the wire lightly. If he didn't touch it at all, he could run even faster. But that meant taking a chance of getting too far from the wire and losing the way.

Ray heard the other children running back and forth, racing. The sound was sharp and clear to his ears. He could tell how far away they ran by their voices. Ray figured the wire was about 100 feet long.

He knew how to measure. He had learned by helping his father build and repair things for neighbors. At first he had been able to see. But later, even when he could no longer see, he had still helped.

His mother did not baby him, either. She gave him
chores to do. One of his chores was to cut wood. He
had to use an ax to do it.

One day some women saw the blind boy chopping
wood with an ax. They were shocked and angry with his
mother. But Ray's mother did not care about them. She
cared about her son. She wanted him to do as much as
he could without help.

"You running, Foots?"

"Yeah," Ray said. His toes dug into the sandy Florida dirt.

"READY, SET, GO!"

Ray started. His hand kept a light touch on the wire. It felt easy.

The running part was easy, too. He was used to racing barefoot across dirt yards. He was always speeding across his own yard at home on his way to his neighbors.

Ray could hear the children shouting. Faster and faster he ran. He was streaking somewhere in the dark and everything was perfect.

He didn't need to see. Not this time. Not now, not ever. He felt great.

Then sudden pain smashed into him.

WHAM!

They had tricked him. There was no child at the other end of the wire. They had tied it to an iron post.

The hurt was too much. Ray started to cry.

"Little baby!" someone yelled. "Little sissy boy!"

Tears tried hard to get past his eyelids. But Ray squeezed his eyelids tighter.

"Foots is a baby!" the children shouted again and again.

Today, the little barefoot boy is a man. He is famous. People don't call him Foots. They call him Ray Charles. The whole world knows him. He is a great musician.

He is still blind, but nobody would dare trick him into hitting an iron post.

Huge crowds of people come to his concerts to see him play the piano and sing. He wears dark glasses and rocks back and forth on the piano stool as his body and soul keep time with the beautiful sound of his voice.

The music of Ray Charles is a mix of many styles, including gospel music and jazz. His music has the power of a story. It tells about love and pain and joy and trouble.

You can hear his tears in it.

Sometimes, when people clap and clap and clap, he gets up from the piano and stands, holding his arms out to them. It makes the people feel good.

Sometimes they cry when he sings about trouble.

Ray Charles Robinson, who was born able to see on September 23, 1930, in Albany, Georgia, knows what trouble is.

Ray Charles calls Greenville, Florida, his home. He went there to live when he was still a baby. There his little brother lived and died. And there his parents, Bailey and Retha Robinson, tried to find doctors to save his eyesight. But it was hard for Black families in the South to get good medical care.

When Ray was six years old, his left eye had to be removed. It was very diseased. A year later his other eye became blind. His mother sent him to St. Augustine School to get the special training he would need.

In 1969, as a famous musician, Ray Charles returned to the school where he had grown up. At a special program he was honored as the most outstanding person ever to attend the school.

But the small boy, standing near an iron post, did not know all this would happen to him.

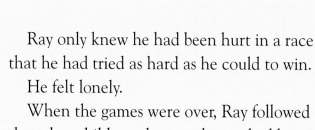

Ray only knew he had been hurt in a race that he had tried as hard as he could to win.

He felt lonely.

When the games were over, Ray followed the other children along paths marked by wire and went back inside the school.

As the days and years passed, it was the school's music classes that Ray grew to love. Music helped him remember home.

Part of remembering home was the old upright piano on the front porch of Mr. Wiley Pitman's house next door.

Ray had not been blind when he first started banging on the old piano. To him, playing a piano was better than fishing and rolling marbles. His bare feet would scramble across to Mr. Pitman's wooden porch as soon as he heard the sound of the piano keys.

Usually the old man kept right on playing. He didn't look up, not even when he felt the little boy climb up on the stool beside him. Mr. Pitman kept a straight face and acted as if Ray's excited fingers, moving back and forth on the keys, were doing all right.

"That's good, Sonny," Mr. Pitman would say to Ray. "That's good."

One day, when Ray was four years old, Mr. Pitman took him to the little cafe he owned.

"Can I play?" Ray begged. "Huh, Mr. Pitman?"

The old man smiled. Finally he said, "Yeah. You can play."

Ray climbed up on the piano bench, in front of all the people sitting around in the cafe, and bammed on the keys over and over again.

That music had been fun. But here at school, music was work. It meant learning to read and write Braille.

Braille is made up of dots pressed out in paper. A blind person can feel these dots with his or her fingers

and read them. Or the person can press out the dots
and write.

Ray learned to read and write music this way. Then
he learned to play every instrument in the school band.

His voice was great. He didn't need to learn to sing.

He would sit at the piano. His fingers would touch
the first note pressed into the paper. Then he would
touch the next note.

He'd play these notes on the piano.

Next, he'd touch four more, play the first two notes,
and add the four new ones.

His fingers would go back and forth from the pushed-
out dots to the piano and back again.

The hardest kind of music for Ray to learn this way was classical. These pieces of music were often pages and pages long.

But Ray knew the kind of music he wanted to play. It was music filled with the great rhythms of Black people. He gave more and more of his time to it. He'd learn a tune and then jazz it up until he had a new sound.

Ray's music got better and better. Soon he was writing Braille arrangements of melodies for bands with as many as 16 or 17 instruments. Ray and some school friends also played music and sang for tea parties and church affairs in town. Ray liked making a few dollars, but most of all he was getting a chance to put his kind of music together.

Then one day, when Ray was 15, a telegram came. It was read to him. His mother had died.

His father and brother were already dead. Ray Charles Robinson was alone. His family was gone.

His sadness was so great that he had to stay in the school hospital for six days.

"After they buried her, I couldn't eat," he said. "I couldn't cry. People kept saying I'd feel better if I could just break down and cry."

But Ray did not break down. Instead, he left school and walked away. He was 15 and blind and without a family. He had a high school diploma. But the most important thing for him was that after hearing a piece of music once he could play it perfectly.

Ray's first job was playing the piano at a radio station.

"I didn't want to spend my life making brooms," he said. "And I didn't want a dog and a cane to get across the street. I wanted to depend on myself."

Ray played with dance bands whenever he could. Sometimes he had to say he was 21 to get into a club. Once he played with a group of men called the Florida Playboys. He had to dress up like a cowboy.

Times were hard and Ray had little money. Sometimes he was paid with food. Often he had only sardines and crackers to eat. Sometimes he had nothing. All he could do then was drink water.

When he was able to get money, Ray spent it carefully. And he saved some. After a while he had saved six hundred dollars.

"What's the farthest place on the map I can go," Ray asked a friend in the band, "and still be in the United States?"

His friend spread his hand over a map. He kept his thumb on Florida. "New York's five inches away."

"Don't want to go to New York," Ray said. "New York's too big."

"Los Angeles is seven inches away."

"Keep going," Ray said.

"You must want Seattle. It's eight inches away from Florida."

"Seattle it is," Ray answered.

"You're crazy," his friend told him. "You're blind *and* crazy!"

But Ray Charles Robinson wasn't crazy. When he arrived in Seattle, Washington, he was 16 years old. He had traveled from one end of the United States to another.

Ray was very tired, but he walked until he found a place to live. It was a rooming house. He got into bed and slept for 18 hours. When he woke up, after midnight, he asked his landlady if any nightclubs were still open.

She said yes. The Rocking Chair was open.

Ray went there and found that they were having a talent show. Ray didn't win the contest. But the club offered him a job playing the piano and singing.

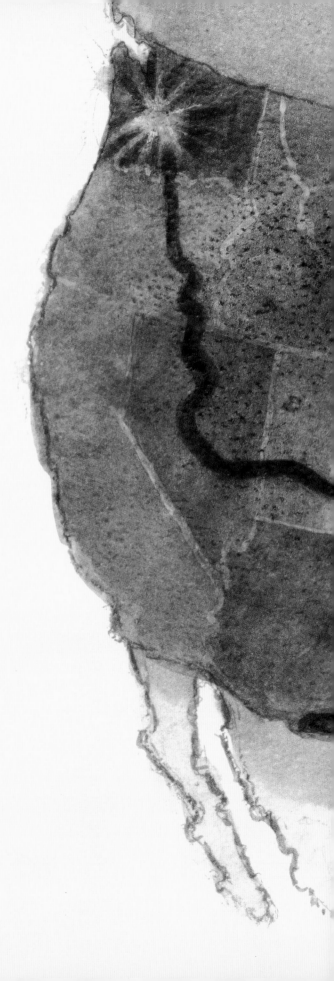

In a few weeks Ray was hired by another club, but he drew in so many people that The Rocking Chair wanted him back. They offered to pay him twice as much money as they had paid him before.

Then some good luck and some bad luck happened to Ray at the same time.

A man from a record company asked if he wanted to make a record. Ray said yes.

There was a musicians' strike going on at the time. It was against union rules to make a record. But Ray went ahead and made the recording anyway.

The union caught him. He had to pay a six-hundred-dollar fine. It took all his money to pay it.

Ray had to start over to save money. He became a sideman, playing the piano and other instruments for the main musician. He did this at several nightclubs. Then in 1948, Ray and two other musicians formed a group called the McSon Trio. The McSon Trio was the first African American act to get its own television show in the Pacific Northwest.

Ray decided to shorten his name from Ray Charles Robinson to Ray Charles. He did not want people to mix him up with the famous boxer Sugar Ray Robinson.

One of the places where Ray Charles sang was the famous Apollo Theatre in Harlem in New York City. Black people lived in Harlem. They loved the Apollo. Many African American stars performed at the Apollo when they first began their careers.

Ray Charles worked harder and harder and kept practicing the music he wanted to play. He would stay up five and six nights in a row playing a piece on the piano until he got the sound he wanted. It took hours more to press out the notes in Braille.

In 1954, Ray hired seven musicians to play the beautiful music he had put together. Many people said it was one of the best jazz groups in the country. Ray Charles played the alto sax and the piano. And he sang.

His voice was soulfully rich and mellow.

Then something wonderful happened. Ray had a hit record! "I Got A Woman," a song he wrote, arranged the music for, and sang, reached the number two spot on Billboard's Rhythm and Blues chart. Soon Ray Charles was very well known.

Soon Ray Charles owned his own record company. He named the company Tangerine after his favorite fruit.

During recording sessions, Ray Charles was a perfectionist. He expected his musicians to play their instruments without making mistakes. He expected his recording engineers to make the sound come out as clear and as true as he wanted it. He expected his singers, the Raelettes, to back him up with pinpoint harmony. Once he told them, "I'm not hard to get along with. . . . I just have to have everything perfect."

People found out how long and hard Ray was willing to work to come up with the exact sound he wanted.

Ray Charles has perfect pitch. Few people have perfect pitch. His ears are so sharp that he can always hear a wrong note. Once he was listening to 30 musicians playing. Suddenly he stopped them. He told one of the violinists he was playing a D-sharp instead of a D-natural. And it was true.

There was a time when the Raelettes couldn't make it to a recording session. Ray Charles put on earphones and sang each woman's part, one at a time.

Ray sang in four different voices. The end result was absolutely flawless. It sounded as if four women were singing along with him.

Ray Charles can do almost anything he likes.

When he wants to play dominoes, he does. In games of chess, his black chess pieces are larger than the white ones. He plays cards with a Braille deck.

How does Ray Charles tell time? He opens the dome of his Braille watch and feels the numbers.

When he wants to, Ray can take apart a tape recorder or a television set. Then he puts it back together again.

Ray Charles has a great deal of money. People spend millions of dollars buying his recordings and going to his

concerts. He has the money to pay people to do everything
for him. But he does not do this.

When he needs clothes, Ray Charles picks them out
himself. He talks with the tailor and decides on the styles
and colors he wants.

"I can tell if I like the material by the way it feels," he says.

Ray feels his new cars, too. He touches the headlights,
doors, windows, windshield, and dashboard. Then he knows
what the car looks like. He test drives his cars, on his own
property, with someone tapping his shoulders to tell him
which way to make turns.

Ray Charles also knows about airplanes. He owned two of them.

"If he could get a license, Ray could fly a plane, too," his pilot said. "He knows what makes a plane tick and what makes it fly."

Once, when his mechanic was unable to fix a bolt on Ray Charles' plane, the blind musician reached up and screwed the bolt in and they were ready to fly.

"He couldn't see it as well as I could feel it," Ray said.

Ray Charles watches television by listening to words and sounds. He goes to football and baseball games. He can even ride a motor scooter, very fast, by following behind another scooter and listening to its sound.

Ray Charles married a beautiful woman named Della. They had three sons, Ray, Jr., David, and Robert. They lived in a large house in Los Angeles. It had a swimming pool shaped like a piano.

"I can't think of anything that means more to me than to go home," Ray would say.

Ray Charles has been called a genius by the music world. He has won some of the highest music awards and honors in the United States and from countries around the world.

Once Ray Charles received something special from African Americans. It was a collection of 8,500 signatures under the heading of one of his most famous songs, "I Can't Stop Loving You." They gave him this because he refused to give a concert in front of a segregated audience in Atlanta, Georgia, where people were not allowed to sit where they wanted because of the color of their skin.

Ray Charles walked out of the auditorium rather than have people
insulted. He had to pay a fine of seven hundred fifty-seven dollars.

Ray Charles loves children. He supports the work of the
National Association for Sickle Cell Disease. Sickle cell disease
affects the blood. Most of its victims are Black children.

Ray Charles remembers what it is to be a child. It was as a child
that he could see.

"I remember certain colors," Ray Charles says. "Red, blue, and yellow. When somebody says 'red hat,' I know what that means. I remember what a lot of things look like. I remember my father's face, my mother's face."

Often it hurts for Ray to remember.

"Sometimes," he says, "when I am singing the blues, I can hardly keep the tears from running down my face. I give it all I got."

It is then that the heavy, throaty voice pours out the trouble he knows. His soul shows, and people see and understand.

And when he bursts into songs of joy, people see that and understand, too.

His voice strains with the words, "It's all right!"

And they know, if he tells them, it *is* all right.

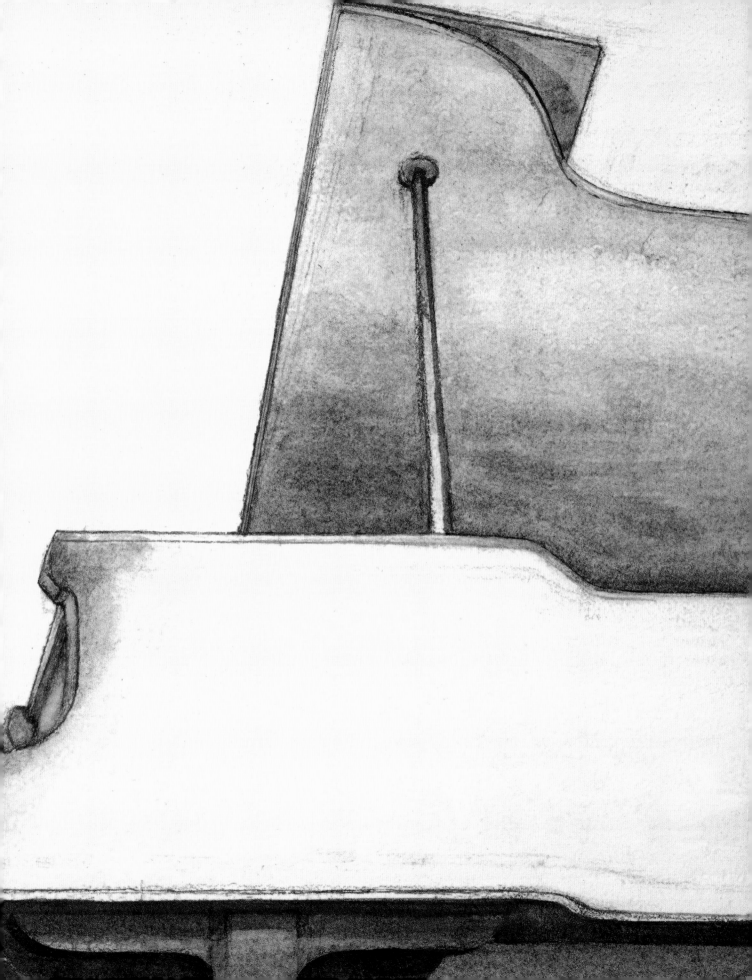

AFTERWORD

TODAY Ray Charles is a legendary musician, a superstar of the entertainment world who has fulfilled his boyhood dream to "be a great musician." He plays the piano, saxophone, clarinet, and organ. He composes and arranges music, and writes and sings songs, too. He has won 12 Grammy Awards for excellence in the music industry and has received numerous awards and honors for his artistic achievements. Ray Charles also appears in movies and on television.

Many of Ray Charles' recordings have sold millions of copies. One of his most popular songs has been "Georgia On My Mind," which was also popular in 1930, the year Ray Charles was born. "Georgia" became his signature song because of the beautiful way he sings the words. In 1979, when "Georgia On My Mind" became the state song of Georgia, Ray Charles was invited to sing it for the Georgia House of Representatives.

Ray Charles is a grandfather. He is no longer married to Della. His record company, Tangerine, is now a division of Ray Charles Enterprises. He has created the Robinson Foundation for Hearing Disorders to help people who are deaf. "My ears tell me 99 percent of what I need to know about my world," Ray Charles says. "My eyes are my handicap, but my ears are my opportunity."

In 1983, Ray Charles was honored by the NAACP's Image Awards. In 1986, President Reagan presented him with the Kennedy Center Honors Medal, the most prestigious award in the entertainment world. Also in 1986, Ray Charles was inducted into the Rock and Roll Hall of Fame even though his music is a blend of jazz, blues, pop, rock, gospel, and country western. And in 1992, President Clinton awarded Ray Charles the National Medal of Arts.

Dreams can come true. Just ask Ray Charles.

S. B. M.